A Little Book of Taiwanese Eats

A Bopomofo Foodie Book

For my daughter Cassidy, so that she may one day love stinky tofu as much as I do. —M.C.

To my Mom, a constant source of love, food, and everything in between. —S.L.

Copyright ©2022 Maryann Chu
New York, NY

All rights reserved. No part of this book may be used or reproduced in any form or by any means- electronic, mechanical, photocopy, recording, or other- without prior written permission from the author.
Written by: Maryann Chu
Illustrated by: Stephany Lai
Designed by: Lucia Benito
Library of Congress Control Number 2022913745
ISBN 978-1-7362852-9-9
Printed in the USA

Author's Note

Mandarin Chinese and Taiwanese Hokkien are two of the most commonly used languages in Taiwan. In this book, most dishes are shown with their Mandarin Chinese pronunciations. A few, however, are shown with their Taiwanese Hokkien pronunciations, as that is what they usually go by.

All the dishes have one thing in common though—they taste delicious!

ㄅ

bào bīng
刨ㄅㄠˋ冰ㄅㄧㄥ
Shaved Ice

Add red beans and taro
and mangos and more
to finely shaved ice—
It's a treat we adore!

Also called "tsuà bīng" in Taiwanese Hokkien.

ㄆ

pí dàn
皮ㄆㄧˊ 蛋ㄉㄢˋ
Century Eggs

With creamy, gray yolk
and a dark amber skin,
each time you eat congee
you'll want it thrown in!

ㄇ

mán　　tou
饅ㄇㄢˊ頭ㄊㄡ
Steamed Buns

This soft, fluffy bun
has a milky-white tone.
We fry it or stuff it—
or eat on its own.

ㄈ

fàn　　tuán
飯ㄈㄢˋ糰ㄊㄨㄢˊ
Sticky Rice Roll

With all sorts of goodies
inside of this roll—
A portable breakfast
to eat as you stroll.

ㄅ

dòu　　huā
豆ㄉㄡˋ花ㄏㄨㄚ
Tofu Pudding

Such soft, silken tofu—
A tasty delight.
With syrup and peanuts . . .
Let's have some tonight!

tāng　yuán

湯圓

Glutinous Rice Balls

These tasty round treats
are made salty or sweet.
On special occasions,
they're ones we might eat!

ㄋ

niú　　ròu　　miàn
牛ㄋㄧㄡˊ肉ㄖㄡˋ麵ㄇㄧㄢˋ
Beef Noodle Soup

This national dish has a broth full of flavor and tender, soft beef that you can't help but savor.

ㄌ

lǔ ròu fàn
滷肉飯
ㄌㄨˇ ㄖㄡˋ ㄈㄢˋ

Braised Pork Rice

A savory, rich mix
made with pork that you braise—
"It melts in your mouth!"
is quite often the praise.

guà   bāo

刈ㄍㄨㄚ 包ㄅㄠ

Pork Belly Buns

A thick slice of pork
that's so rich and so tender
inside a white bun—
A "best sandwich" contender!

* "Guà bāo" is the Taiwanese Hokkien name for this dish.

kǎo yù mǐ
烤玉米
Taiwanese Grilled Corn

Well-coated with soy sauce
plus garlic and more,
like corn on the cob,
but with sauces galore!

huǒ guō
火ㄏㄨㄛˇ 鍋ㄍㄨㄛ
Hot Pot

Around a large pot filled with boiling hot soup—
Dip meats and some veggies and eat as a group.

ㄑ

qǐ　sī　mǎ　líng　shǔ
起ㄑㄧˇ司ㄙ馬ㄇㄚˇ鈴ㄌㄧㄥˊ薯ㄕㄨˇ
Cheese Potato

Potatoes are mashed
and then breaded outside.
They're topped with hot cheese . . .
And what else? You decide!

T

xiāng　cháng
香腸
Taiwanese Sausages

These Taiwanese sausages
taste a bit sweet.
With zesty raw garlic,
the flavor's complete.

zhēn zhū nǎi chá
珍珠奶茶
Boba Milk Tea

This sweet, milky drink that is made with black tea has chewy, round bobas inside that are key!

chòu　dòu　fu

臭ㄔㄡˋ豆ㄉㄡˋ腐ㄈㄨ˙
Stinky Tofu

You'll smell this great dish from a whole mile away. "You'll love it or hate it!" is what people say.

ㄕ

shāo bǐng
燒(ㄕㄠ) 餅(ㄅㄧㄥ)
Sesame Flatbread

Some sesame seeds
top this flaky, baked bread.
It's best filled with egg—
or with beef, some have said.

ròu　　yuán
肉ㄖㄡˋ圓ㄩㄢˊ
Taiwanese Meatball

With savory stuffings like pork and bamboo, there's chewy, clear skin you can almost see through!

Also called "bà wán" in Taiwanese Hokkien.

ㄗ

zòng　　zi
粽ㄗㄨㄥˋ 子ㄗ˙
Sticky Rice Dumpling

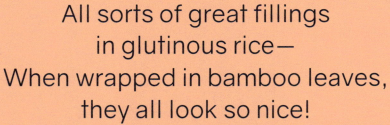

All sorts of great fillings
in glutinous rice—
When wrapped in bamboo leaves,
they all look so nice!

ㄘ

cōng　yóu　bǐng
蔥ㄘㄨㄥ 油ㄧㄡˊ 餅ㄅㄧㄥˇ
Scallion Pancake

Soft dough mixed with scallion
is flattened and fried . . .
A rich, crispy texture
each time we have tried.

sān bēi jī
三杯雞
Three-Cup Chicken

A dish made with chicken inside a clay pot is cooked with three sauces and served piping hot.

Y

tián　bú　là
甜不辣
Taiwanese Fish Cake

It's made out of fish paste
that's boiled and then fried—
In all shapes and sizes,
with sauce on the side.

ㄛ

This herb-flavored rice cake has fillings inside,
like radish that's shredded and shrimp that's been dried.

ài cǎo guǒ
艾ㄞˋ草ㄘㄠˇ粿ㄍㄨㄛˇ

Mugwort Rice Cake

* Also called "tsao ah kuèh" in Taiwanese Hokkien.

uh ah jiān

蚵ㄜˊ仔ㄚˋ煎ㄐㄧㄢ

Oyster Omelet

So gooey and chewy
and savory-sweet—
The oysters are plump
in this night market treat.

* *"uh ah jiān"* is the Taiwanese Hokkien name for this dish.

fān shǔ yè

蕃ㄈㄢ 薯ㄕㄨˇ 葉ㄧㄝˋ

Sweet Potato Leaves

Delicious and healthy,
this green, heart-shaped leaf—
When stir-fried with garlic,
it's tasty! Good grief!

ㄞ

ài　　yù
愛ㄞˋ玉ㄩˋ
Aiyu Jelly

This natural clear jelly
you eat many ways.
With lime and some syrup,
it's best on hot days.

lǔ wèi

滷味
Lu Wei

From fish cake and seaweed
to tofu and meat—
They're stewed in some spices,
then chopped up to eat.

ㄠ

xiǎo　　lóng　　bāo

小ㄒㄧㄠˇ 籠ㄌㄨㄥˊ 包ㄅㄠ

Soup Dumplings

These delicate dumplings
are steamed in bamboo—
With tasty meat fillings
and soup inside, too!

ㄩ

yù　tou　gāo
芋ㄩˋ頭ㄊㄡˊ糕ㄍㄠ

Taro Cake

There's taro and shrimp
and some pork in this cake.
But make no mistake . . .
You must steam it—not bake!

ㄢ

guān cái bǎn
棺ㄍㄨㄢ 材ㄘㄞˊ 板ㄅㄢˇ
Coffin Bread

First scoop a deep hole in a thick slice of bread. Add creamy, hot soup and consider me fed!

ㄏ

huā　　shēng　　bīng　　qí　　lín
花ㄏㄨㄚ 生ㄕㄥ 冰ㄅㄧㄥ 淇ㄑㄧˊ 淋ㄌㄧㄣˊ

Peanut Ice Cream Roll

It's nutty and creamy,
this ice cream burrito.
The added cilantro,
some eat and some veto!

ㄤ

dòu　　jiāng
豆ㄉㄡˋ漿ㄐㄧㄤ
Soy Milk

This popular drink
that is made out of soy—
Served hot or ice cold . . .
Either way, you'll enjoy!

hú jiāo bǐng
胡ㄏㄨˊ椒ㄐㄧㄠ餅ㄅㄧㄥˇ
Pepper Pork Buns

There's peppery pork
in this round, flaky bun.
Inside a clay oven
it's baked till it's done.

mù ěr
木耳
Wood Ear Mushroom

They're dark brown in color and often sold dried, but springy and crunchy when water's applied!

一

yóu   tiáo
油condition 條ㄊㄧㄠˊ
Fried Dough Stick

This tasty, fried dough is so crispy and hot. It's eaten with soy milk or congee a lot!

fèng lí sū
鳳ㄈㄥˋ梨ㄌㄧˊ酥ㄙㄨ
Pineapple Cake

There's pineapple filling that's hidden inside this buttery pastry that's gifted with pride.

ㄩ

yù　　yuán
芋ㄩˋ 圓ㄩㄢˊ
Taro Balls

This taro dessert
you'll enjoy through and through—
So bouncy and chewy,
we say it's "Q-Q."

About the Author

Maryann Chu is a Taiwanese-American author from New York. Some of her happiest memories are of her travels to Taiwan—visiting relatives, exploring the island, and getting lost in night markets. She is a frequent eater of all things Taiwanese, from the stinkiest of tofus to the beefiest of noodle soups.

Maryann currently lives in New York City with her husband and daughter, and her favorite dish is Braised Pork Rice.

For more books by Maryann, visit:

Website: www.ourlittlemando.com

Instagram: @ourlittlemando

About the Illustrator

Stephany Lai grew up in San Diego, spending many summers visiting her large extended family back in Taiwan. Her path through art was partly inspired by her grandfather, a traditional nihonga (膠彩畫) artist in Taipei. Now, she uses digital illustrations to share her vibrant Taiwanese-American culture with the world.

Stephany currently lives in San Francisco, and her favorite dish is Taiwanese Shaved Snow.

For more art by Stephany, visit:

Instagram: @laiberry.art

Made in United States
Cleveland, OH
11 October 2024